BELATED BRIS OF THE B

BELATED BRIS
OF THE BRAINSICK

LUCAS
CRAWFORD

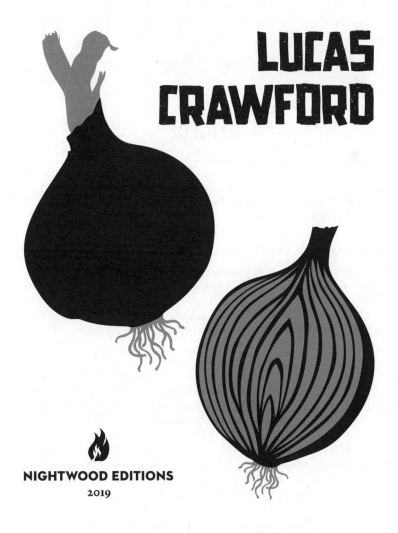

NIGHTWOOD EDITIONS

2019

Nightwood Editions
P.O. Box 1779
Gibsons, BC VON 1VO
Canada
www.nightwoodeditions.com

COVER DESIGN & TYPOGRAPHY: Carleton Wilson

Nightwood Editions acknowledges the support of the Canada Council for the Arts, which last year invested $153 million to bring the arts to Canadians throughout the country.

Nous remercions le Conseil des arts du Canada de son soutien. L'an dernier, le Conseil a investi 153 millions de dollars pour mettre de l'art dans la vie des Canadiennes et des Canadiens de tout le pays.

We also gratefully acknowledge financial support from the Government of Canada and from the Province of British Columbia through the BC Arts Council and the Book Publishing Tax Credit.

This book has been produced on 100% post-consumer recycled, ancient-forest-free paper, processed chlorine-free and printed with vegetable-based dyes.

Printed and bound in Canada.

LIBRARY AND ARCHIVES CANADA CATALOGUING IN PUBLICATION

Title: Belated bris of the brainsick / Lucas Crawford.
Names: Crawford, Lucas, author.
Description: Poems.
Identifiers: Canadiana (print) 20190089369 | Canadiana (ebook) 20190089393 |
ISBN 9780889713666 (softcover) | ISBN 9780889713673 (ebook)
Classification: LCC PS8605.R43 B45 2019 | DDC C811/.6—dc23

CONTENTS

3. *Crazy in Love*

1.

BELATED BRIS

PICK YOUR POISON, OR, "AGENCY"

You've gotta take a bath, m'dear!
So what'll it be: toy boat or bath beads?
This shirt or that? Frat or sorority?
Getting fresh or canned? Marching
band or the rugby squad? Salisbury
mistake or the over-overdone cod?

Now or later, either/or, more or less.
Confess or BURN! Gordon Korman
or *Where the Red Fern Grows*?
Prose or poetry, science or art? Fart
or hold it (just for fun). Italics
or **bold** (Choose. One.). Comic Sans
or Papyrus; it's so funny to know
there's no life without this virus.

M psych ward roommate or *F*?
Bibliography or References?
I am not the source. But so glad
you asked about my preferences.

BECOMING MISCHLING OF THE SECOND DEGREE
ON SUICIDAL CHRISTMAS

Mischling of the second degree:

*A person with one Jewish grandparent; "mischling" is from the
German for "mixed," "half-breed"; what I am (a fact learned in my
early thirties); something hidden in a tangle of abuse, booze, anti-
Semitism, poverty and lies—knotted rosary beads sunk to the bottom
of a rum tumbler; constitutive absence; the inscrutable wound over
which I ran my tongue; the silence around which life was structured.*

I.

My new name tag reads like a crime
and I know that's a full sentence
even if my creed is inconsistency
Hi My Name Is… Mixed Feelings!

Nanny. A man named Block and she committed me in 1953.
I was not premeditated but their hot want
ought to stand up as malice aforethought.
Reckless engenderment of bastard granddaughter [sic]

but it took sixty-two years for them to get caught
between the sheets of their Liverpool Street sin. Are they
the syncopation in the beat to which I tap my feet
as I imagine life as a bail session from which to abscond?

At the bank trading in papyrus bonds
jaundiced babies point to me.
I'm mischling of the second degree
which means I'm not, legally, blond.

Punishment is time severed, guillotined hands
and heads, or the busted bamboo knots that bind
wrists to beds if one refuses one's meds
or writes too many singsong rhymes.

Too many times we have been belated.
When he died, I started wearing Dad's watch
until the strap broke and it got lost.
Idle hands operate on mundane memories:

How I could never hula-hoop. Afternoons walking
the track. A life-sized motorized Santa Claus
of which only its pelvis moved. Air Cadet weekends
tucked into a Windsor Park barrack three blocks

from where my father was conceived. Do the things
from which people protect you tend to be the very things
you need? Then, an interruption—impromptu college
lecture on criminal obstruction and the concept of *mens rea*.

The PowerPoint says: CECI N'EST PAS UN "POWERPOINT,"
but: For the mid-term exam, brainstorm a theory of life
as the hardest, drunk scavenger hunt that [never] ends
with the onion-skin myth of pearl-pure intent.

II.

Santa comes down the chimney and I vanish
up it in a cloud of self-smoke. He calls his alternate

troupe of elves who wear brown shirts
and keep stricter lists than their merry master.

I become the hot puff that beckons
the neighbour kid's asthmatic lung from within.

Soon, coal will be the most prized gift
♫ *You don't know what you've got 'til it's soot* ♫

I steal a look into Santa's sac of loot: an alp
of children's shoes, one stuffed with cold foot,

a sit-in of dolls with eyes that don't close,
a mint of necklaces that could dry-drown any digger,

grave- or gold-. Busy urban laundry room
on Christmas so we go for a swim on the third floor.

My friend pushes for the sauna. I say, *Just a few
minutes more?* For, I have always panicked in steam

rooms with those fuming showerheads and heart-
heavy doors the non-existent locks of which I am certain

will malfunction. My head is a mimetically sealed
chamber I'd shut down if only learning I'm Jewish(ish)

could have killed my catholic(ick) compunction.
A performance artist once sliced onions with strangers

until they could stop, be held and cry. Sentiment:
another airborne disease to pantomime

over salted-maple pecan pie and no-whip chai?
I stick sweetly to the words that sorrow whispers

into my thighs with perfect elocution: you may know
the problem. You are ~~not not~~ not the final solution.

III.

Just a list of clichés about my cheap selfhood
clattering like drunk Yahtzee or Boggle or Trouble

or another game that's louder than *les manifestations
casseroles*. Dice fall out with no black dots.

Boggle's cubes settle down but show only *Qu*,
X, *W* and other dead letters. In the mirror

I see professional photographers whose boon was 2002.
Getty Images must have hired them to retake

stock photos of Manhattan air; I double-dog dared
myself to snap a still pre-pill with morning hair—

to take a picture that aims to conceal what only used to be
there. The security guard says I am too fat to sit

on a painted pony that does not move. Another
mirror shows me the abandoned scaffolding

of the most recently failed Oak Island treasure hunt.
As I fall, may the skyline look like an architectural

kaleidoscope. May I not have to remember Mies
van der Rohe or bad trips. May I fall asleep

on the way down to make the euphemizing
of my eulogy and obituary easier. "He died peacefully

in his sleep, surrounded by the wet-grey concrete
modernism about which he felt ambivalent at best."

May I dream in that cattiest of naps that we had all
risked more. That my Jewish dad might have reached

down to me, honked my schnoz and flipped
a kid script, taunting: *You've got my nose.*

OBITUARY

I would never write an obituary ahead of time.
It would be written badly, adjective- and adverb-
weighted to anchor you (or you) inkly to the ground.
Self-fulfilling prof, you see? (Apologies.)

My obit will not place paper dolls over wet wounds,
will unravel a skein of shimmering yarn
over the hay shirt I was fitted for long, too long, ago,
Scaredy-crow. Let my drafts of auto-death-prose

go. Let them fail to decompose. Let them heart-harden
to papier-mâché. Let me trip on this mummy on a grey
gentile holiday, nutcrack it open to find inside
burnt kernels of you. Those are for the chemists

to investigate while I open, close, open, close
the blinds like you used to do. Let me pretend
to live inside your old, jammed viewfinder.
I wrote your obituary ahead of time.

Do you remember my catatonic fall? Sundays
were the scoop-shop outing for I the infirm.
Mom and I talked about loving *Annie Hall*.
(The thought that she'd seen it was uncanny.

As the Moon Mist melted, it sunk in.
She meant *Annie*.) It's a hard knock life
not wanting to be part of any club
that would have you as a member.

*In someone's obit I have asterisked this
as the ideal time at which I would have been told
I'm Jewish. But tricky us, we wait
for tomorrow, tomorrow, transplendent

tomorrow. The Kafkaesque is only a day
away… I wrote an obit on the back
of a collage of Keith's labels held together
with holy water and melted butter,

even if some things just don't mix. The lobster's
already dead behind the fridge, hollow shell
lack-blue. Are you empty too, your liver
flown the coop, your heart martyred off

into a collection plate, or split in two,
then two, then two? No? I'll wait. Premature
obits have no expiration date. You're not
a celebrity but I don't want to write in haste.

Do you ever wonder what a person would
act like who was literally *full* of grace?
My church is high-camp pleasure and low-
grade pain. When I'm laid at last, chain

my brain to the gates of the Home for the Godless
Insane. Stitch me a yellow star out of alternating
rosary and anal beads. This plan has just one hitch:
♫ *You're from the 70s and I'm a 90s bitch* ♫

Our niche is failing to fit and we try to be
too legit for the genre of pre-pre-writ obit.

WE'S THE B'YS

I's the b'y that builds the boat
And I's the b'y that sails her
I's the b'y that catches the fish
And brings them home to Liza.
– "I's the B'y," a Newfoundland folk song

I.

I's the b'y who's a secret Jew
and I's the b'y who wore an xxs yarmulke.
I's the b'y who Dad carried on his shoulders
at the beach, and whose face, framed,
hung on his boarding-room wall.
I's the b'y who was retrieved one day.

I's the b'y who's back with his mother
and new scum stepdad. I's the b'y
fed ketchup sandwiches and knuckle blood,
and the worst part is that I love her.
I's a b'y who you might call a straight white man
I's a b'y whose mother tried to crack a rock
over my head at ten because I was fat.

I's a b'y who left at seventeen
when a beating took my high-pitched hearing,
and then dropped out of high school
'cause there was no bus there from my sister's.
I's the b'y who doesn't know why I get so tan
in the summer that customers call me *mulatto*.

20

I's the b'y flummoxed my frizzy coif wouldn't
fall flat into hip, long locks in the seventies.
I's the b'y who was born a few years
after the Holocaust and who never knew
that I didn't know why I'm this, and this,
and this. I's the b'y who gave an old bastard
CPR at my post office job today
and I's the b'y who couldn't save him.

I's the b'y you'd see as a false-consciousness
idiot who doesn't understand my own
experience because I'm too busy attaining
the crass capital required to buy blood
pudding and potatoes, as if your fucking
hummus is a cloud of angel fart descended
from on high, but who you could probably
learn to fetishize if someone told you
I was the union's vice president and that
I spray-painted placards with stencils
in the lower basement where I rolled
my Belvederes and prepared to strike—

I's a b'y who had two kids. I's the b'y
who never told them they're Jewish-ish.
I's the b'y who visited the sins everywhere.
I's hurting. I's the b'y who died
in my forties before any story shook out.

II.

I's the b'y that moved away and I's the b'y
that visits sometimes. I's the b'y grieving
for the queer metropoles who, hating,
might see nothing but hate in you.

I's the b'y that moved away to Alberta
but not to Fort Mac. I's the b'y called *dyke*
and *faggot* back to back because I's the bi
who ain't a b'y or I's the dude trying to abide
with me, buying a double Kahlúa
with iced chai, marshmallow buoy.

I's the b'y who got pounded in the chest
by a seventh grader for being annoying.
I's the b'y who felt guilty about the green
grapefruit bruise. I's the b'y who kept it
from Mom 'cause feeling guilty
was my dirty habit.

I's the b'y who noticed two of my married,
elementary school teachers were fucking
and I's the b'y who avoided them as much
as possible. I's the b'y one of them fixated on
the term before she took her sick leave.

I's the b'y who always knew my dad hated
holidays and I's the b'y who couldn't figure
out why. I's the b'y whose dad had eight(?)
happy Hanukkahs and forty confusing
Christmases that oscillated between parties
of pepperoni and marble cheese trays,

and playing Santa at the fire hall, or picking
any fight he could at home to break up
the gaiety. Now I hold this photo of him
at four in his bowtie and yarmulke, decanter
of Manischewitz by his tent-pole, teenaged
brother—and the I in I's has always been
the most controversial pronoun.

I's the b'y who can't sleep in Vancouver
and I's the b'y who feels unentitled to write
about my uncanny coast. I's the b'y who
fucking does it anyway because it turns out
that tea *was* caffeinated and today *was*
the seventh grey day of clichéd rain.

I's the b'y leaning east like a flower
that can't reach the window. Godless
waters and abandoned mines, this place
is hardly the molten core of hegemony,
even with these mixed metaphors
which is not to abdicate responsibility,
but is to say that the salt of the earth
is also the salt in your wound, and salt
will cure any flesh with time, but perhaps
even that alchemy fights us; "It's a wet
cold," after all, and nothing doing
with bacteria and moisture and hell,
I don't know how anyone kept kosher
around here but speaking of moisture,
we cry holy water or is it a dead sea,
and if so, why aren't we floating, fat belly
up, next to the cod with cartoon *X*s
on their closed eyelids and hey do fish *have*

eyelids that help them not to see, not to be
exposed to my early-morning foggy
memory of he and me, and, of what,
on a rounder earth, could be—?

TELEPHONE GAMES

Tell the worms my dad's not kosher. Tell the rabbi that the salt's not pure. Tell the sea that its jellyfish sting. Tell the grape jelly it's out of thin style. Tell Coco Chanel that more can be more. Tell Thomas More there are no martyrs in utopia. Tell your favourite saint that they had good PR. Tell a spin doctor to prescribe you a vinyl cure. Tell a broken record to stop crying. Tell a stop sign to go to hell. Tell the fire it's got nothing on you. Tell yourself to live in a tree. Tell the tree to go back to its roots. Tell the roots to look around. Tell the ground to hold fast to its worms. Tell the worms my dad's not kosher. Tell my dad he's set beneath a stone. Tell the stone I'll get its sword. Tell the knight I won't take his word. Tell your words to go back to the dictionary. Tell your dictionary that you need a break. Tell your break that this is a breakdown. Tell your breakdown to wait. Tell the waiting room about your grocery list. Tell the Sobeys flier that you need dulse. Tell your dulse to season your dinner. Tell your dinner guests that the meat doesn't need salt. Tell the salt it's not pure. Tell the pure they incubate dead lies. Tell your lies to your rabbi. Tell your kosher grocer to warn the worms. Tell the worms my dad's not kosher. Tell the small yarmulke it didn't fit. Tell your Fitbit to read about cyborgs. Tell your cyborg self the nineties still matter. Tell Carrie Bradshaw you couldn't help but wonder. Tell your Wonder Bread it needs peanut butter and apple jelly. Tell the jellyfish they make the ocean sting. Tell Sting that he can't tell Roxanne what dress to not put on. Tell Roxanne not to call the police. Tell the police not to stand so close to me.

PSYCH WARD GRUB

I'm the choosy beggar
with a Ph.D. and wet bare feet.
I don't want cold cream of wheat
or sour lukewarm honeydew.
I want a world of the curly-coiffed
trucker who offered me half
his lunch because I was new.

I don't want the cornstarch-slurried
puddle of paltry "stew" that would
make a fine papier-mâché
scented with *eau-de-poulet*.
(Are *you* chicken?)

I want the spike of every Louboutin
sidewalk-splashing in Vancouver
to be auctioned off by a nurse
who speaks off-brand-table-syrup
slow and calls me "dear."
Proceeds would supply psych wards
with berries, Twix, spices and chips—
in perpetuity (which is to say,
year after year after...)

The last time I ate flesh so hard,
I was kneeling for communion,
a young gun dreaming of Funyons
just to Pavlov's-dogs that dry
wafer down. Now is the revival:
imagining pink Jolly Ranchers
just to psych up my saliva.

So please don't balk when I say,
I WANT SOME FUCKING SALT.
Sodium chloride? Nacl? *Sel de mer*?
Yes, freshly cracked, crunchy
and coarse… Mrs. Dash?
MRS. DASH? The word that comes
to mind, Madame, is *divorce*.

Due to irreconcilable similarities
to the colour of human waste,
I don't want to choose
between this pabulum or that one.
I wish my tablemate would stop
calling me fat, but when I was crying
and offered him Sun Chips, he said,
I've got your back, brother.

Did you know there are professors
who proclaim that tough men
know no tender feelings? At tea time,
we bleed Red Rose, but where's
the chai, the Earl Grey, the Darjeeling?

From the "ketchup is a vegetable"
file, one might ask: Is an appetizer
of cranberry cocktail
known to promote healing?

No.

So,

we need a psych ward 500+ item buffet!

ALL YOU CAN EAT IF YOU LIVE
ONE MORE DAY (now with sundae bar)

I want every Acadienne to spread
into the thick bliss of buttered rappie
pie. The old-timer who has never left
her zombie town might not die
if she had sushi to try, pad Thai wok-fried,
or Montreal bagels. (Hush, New York,
take it in stride.) What else?
I don't know… Nanaimo bars
made in a dive bar in Nanaimo?

In lieu of a menu, there'll be a petition
to sign, to be sent to the Gastronomati.
It will demand that the word "forage"
be proprietary to those who sniff out
hospital storage in order to
(with plastic spoon, crackers and sludge)
scavenge their way to a passable porridge.
It's semi-homemade *and* lean! Call it
"Sandra Lee Meets Rene Redzepi" cuisine.

No disrespect to the meat loaf machine,
that surgical-steel beef guillotine,
the aloof silver tooth that pre-portions
us from on high. Far be it from I
not to give my atheist thanks
to the underpaid ranks who shepherd
any grub here. I worship thee,
sacrificial spam on prodigal bun.
But my fruit cocktail came back up

ipecac-quick, and now I can only eat
these words for fun.

My cohorts on the ward are mostly poor,
mostly white, some homeless, and might not
be well-versed in appropriation debates.

      Would you deny a schizo a schnitzel
if it extended her expiration date?
      Would you refuse a California roll
to my electroshocked friend with the shakes?
(The rice *would* be gummy and the crab
would be fake. But if *this* is where
you'd police food, find another hot take.)
      We. Are. All. Flawed. And charmed.
      But could you call my friends lucky?
      Would you let them eat cake?

It hurts here. Bruised clingstone brain.
It hurts here. We eat swill then try
not to shit shame. We are very different,
but our farts all smell the same.

Excuse me—

Until the utopian buffet opens
I'll be here rocking in my bed, cradling
a plastic ladle, remembering chili,
chowder and daal. Repeating
one thing over and over until I'm free
of good-stew withdrawal.

No, I'll say it 'til it's fucking foodie
folklore: the food in the psych ward
must be ~~to die~~ to live for.

INJURY

I've slipped out of my skin yet you twist a pin in.
It's banana-peeling somewhere, my slapstick
cocoon, black-fleck bruised, tripping you.

Up your feet fly from my hide while I learn to cry
without eyelids, wipe my ass, form a frown.
I've slipped out my skin and I'm playing

my organs all over downtown for free
but I could use a tip or two for the purpose
of buying another wind in which to spin

for a while, of learning how to put on old clothes,
of obtaining a skin graft for my thumb
so I can stick it out and move myself a mile

or two in my own or other shoes, or in anything
else that laces me up so my blubber can sit still
at your staid supper, kind host, rather than

rupturing over your gunmetal-done roast.
Rapture! Hup! Tally ho! May my skinless, boneless
breasts not melt like secret schmaltz atop

your pagan potatoes. May my gloveless hands
not bleed as I hand you, to eat, the sour-sweet,
pickled beets. *Mother-pucker!* May all your meats

be replete with the marbling of my callus-free
feet, size 9E!E!E!, if there was such a width
for my girth, a butterfly-bed for my berth at sea,

a certificate so signed for my delivery. My skin
hides. It lives in the Cosine of Trigonometry.
It knows how to work the angles. It's all

square roots and the rest of me is not formulaic.
I multiply myself by one every morning
in order to persist. Even my cells have started

meeting up without me, blocs and cysts,
and they don't let me meddle. They have atypical
rhythms that invite heavy metal and fetal

compositions. (The klutz-clever tempo
of my Ceilidh-Klezmer.) I tap my phantom
heel to find a beat but I only mishear an old EKG

machine's *beep, beep, beeeeeeeeeeeeeeeeeeeeeeeeps.*
I rest only in pieces, as wholes don't know
what they don't know they don't know.

We reap what we throw away and perhaps
my skin will boomerang back "home." This is
not a metaphor. This is not a riddle. I am dying

inside and they're going to peel open my middle.
I've already slipped out of my skin. You twist
a pin in. They will turn me over and over

to appraise the damage. Will they be impressed
by what I've managed to half-bandage?
Will they feel that these dings and digs

have not been so little? They will run
my skin up an Inverness flagpole mouthing,
There's nothing less fit than a fiddle.

BRICKLAYING

When my father was alive, his second-best friend was a bricklayer named Al.

Al lived in the crook of the crescent on which I grew up, in a brick house he built. Al never knocked when he visited; he would burst through our front door without warning, and any young girl who may have been assembling a snack before creeping back to her room to sit on her pillow to revise brooding gay-girl poems could be assured that Al would barge in with all the fanfare of Ed McMahon but *sans* cheque. If Dad and Al went downstairs, I could sneak a snack without my father morphing into a carnival trickster who, instead of guessing my current weight, predicted what my weight would be at certain points in my future. *Step right up* to the fridge and be met with the crystal ball of heavy hope.

If Dad and Al were threesomed by Captain Morgan, I might have heard Dad mention his youth. I'd hear him expound, with a grin, on the impoverished meals he ate as a kid, especially "ketchup sand-wiches!" Why so much joy, I wondered, on these sardonyx-scarce occasions during which he'd permit himself the retrospective view?

To explain, I'd need to talk about bricklaying. Al redid our chim-ney once, and Dad helped redo Al's lawn by driving up to Ayles-ford and getting some quality fertilizer and spreading that shit all over. The neighbourhood was one of friendships between dads who were often openly silly together. There was the trophy they made for whoever grew the biggest pumpkin each year, and there was the time they hauled Dad's three-hundred-pound entry onto a truck bed to drive it to the Howard Dill Pumpkin Growing Competition in Windsor.

It is so easy, when attempting to write of bricklaying, to end up writing about pounds.

What I have to say about bricklaying is that I love cake. Snacker from the start, cake caught on with me like the blazes Dad and Al would beat back annually as members of the volunteer force. Another thing about bricklaying: I love *all cake*.

Chocolate cake
Black Forest cake
Hummingbird cake
Chocolate-chocolate cake
Chocolate-chocolate-chocolate-chocolate-chocolate cake
Kinda Bland Birthday Cake
Cake that says *eat me*
Salted caramel cake
Cake on a plate
Layer cake
Free cake
Cake!

A Recipe for Layer Cake: make a thick sludge out of butter, vanilla and icing sugar. Slice the cake into layers. Stack them up, using the icing to glue them together. Voila, we're talking about bricklaying, and make sure to poke a toothpick into the centre.

One year, on my father's birthday, the neighbourhood adults gathered at Al's for a party. The cake was placed prominently on the snack table for the duration, moated by party platters, each compartment filled with sliced pepperoni, marble cheese, jarred olives, pickles, crackers and Lunenburg pudding. Dad's birthday was two days before Christmas, so the icing was probably elf-green, likely purchased in tubs at Foodland on Main Street (which closed when the owner hung himself over the produce).

I don't think Dad liked holidays much. I learned recently that he was Jewish. Oh, did I already tell you that? Half his youth, he had Hanukkahs with a foster clan. Retrieved by his (ungentle gentile) mother at the age of ten, he was to be the Jewish punching bag of his new stepfather, who had not any pre-nuptial knowledge of my dad's existence. I don't think Dad liked Christmas. No fucking wonder.

Back at his birthday party, everyone leaned forward toward the cake, singing. He blew out the candles and started to slice. *Wait! The knife won't move!* Dad steadied his hand and tried again. No dice, or rather no cake, and no eating it too.

HOLY SHIT, the cake is made outta concrete!

(LAUGHTER.)

Al must be eighty now and still lives in the crook of Matthews Lane. In a box in his basement under dust and covered with sugar-smears hardened like bone char, is a concrete cake.

I like all manner of desserts, really.
Concrete cake
Maple-bacon what-the-fucks
Sweet kugel
Moon mist
Sufganiyot
Oatcakes
Rugelach
Grape nut

Babka
Grunt
Gelt

On television, Michelin-lauded pastry chefs say that a difficult dessert can sense fear and will react accordingly. Soufflé slumps; cream puffs deflate. What does a birthday cake sense, and what must one do if it has the inclination to turn to rock? Watch *The Sword in the Stone* in reverse and listen for references to Satan or buttercream or me.

WELCOME

Glad you have a new kitchen
in which to contemplate death.

Who did the backsplash.
Are those subway tiles.

Will the marble betray
your sanguine stains.

      Doctor said to rest my throat and
      the glissando of question marks.

      Certainty, I have heard, drops off colder—
      drunk baritone soft-shoeing on drab wharf.

Please come in.
Can I offer you some wine

or a hot deal on a burial plot
on the hillside; great view.

Let's taste decaying matter (wine,
cheese, sour cream or spleen).

Let's roast meat in the new gas oven.
The sales boy swore it would self-clean.

      Do not hold a Plath-match
      to their Beaujolais breath.

Enjoying the new kitchen?
Contemplating death?

HOSPITALS

Please, will you tell me again, officer?
Why your dog had to tooth through
his plaid shirt? How his no-weapon
still gave you a scare? Why you suck
on your selfhood like wet air?

Please, will you tell me again, why
do you frown when this reminds him
of OD'd friends? Giggle when he denies
a needle's cool? Lecture him when he
starts to speak of residential school?

Please, tell me why, when she touches
the door, someone pushes some buttons
and some men drop her to the floor
and tranquilize her? Are you sad
that this doesn't surprise her?

Will you tell me, sir, how we got this far?
Why am I in the back seat of your car?

Please, nurse, will you explain why
I cannot talk to her about the poetry slam?
Make plans for us to perform together?
I look for weeks, eastside, but she's ether.

Nurse, I know that I know nothing, but
why is this guy being released this morning?
He spits out his pills and seems buckshot-
gone. He has no home, wants to camp
on my (non-existent) lawn.

Please, sir, tell me how your egg sandwich
tastes after you've strapped down a teen,
put her in place while she screams
that this is just like her last rape.
Does it taste hard-boiled, cold-blooded,

just right? Please help, please help, if you
know how. An officer is removing you now.

GROCERY SHOPPING

Our eyes click together with such force that I almost hear it
happen—like glass-bottled catsup smithereened and bleeding

out on the floor. I've never gotten groceries on this side
of the river before. I'm afraid I won't float. I'm afraid I'll drift

downstream. I'm afraid I'm a daft first-draft dream.
But today I made it on a raft of capsules and tears,

Mr. Stranger-I-Recognize-Here.
Why do I know your eyes, dear?

Were you laid off on a whim by a prim politician? Did you ask
me to sign your pink-slip petition? If I had surgery once,

were you the fat fly in the inky incision? Were you the doc
in silver Birkenstocks and violet scrubs? Did we meet

at the Bear & Cub mixer, and, if so, are you the oil-sands
electrician who bought me a cranberry spritzer?   Oh!

It hits us both. We nod. I walk on. Pick a pumpkin, appraise
a gourd, act bored. But I'm juice-sticky floored (cringe):

you were the intake nurse who supervised my midnight
disrobement in the acute section of the psych ward.

You pulled the curtain closed formally, as if the magic tricks
of the naked sick need cover. What did you see

when you sawed me in half? Did you feel you were stripping
an orange of pith, a banana of peel? You watched me

disrobe to my birthday-suit buck. You watched my surprise
with feigned-bored blue eyes when you wished me

good luck. You watched my pierced nipples flop
onto my bulky belly, my sore hip trip me up. You said

I couldn't keep my tampons. Not even a Diva Cup.
You said they'd give me whatever I needed.

There was no purpose in arguing that I'm a guy who,
indeed, bleeds. Here is where even underwear is a frill.

You took my dirty panties while I brainstormed a will.
You held out two battered blue robes to wrap each

hefty half of me. It was like a consensual striptease danced
to Celine Dion in a land of *francophonie*. But flip

the capitalist script because you are paid to see, paid
to see, to see me. You left. Your two a.m. shadow,

eyes of Curaçao. I rolled, I bled in bed, but I slept, somehow.
I woke to hard yolks. Here is where breakfast

is two eggs served with three spoons. *Now eat!*
(Here is where they imagine a plastic knife could dig six feet.)

Now we are choosing fruit. We both have all our duds on.
Next week I'm packing up my house and sailing the Hudson.

You were a nice guy for a voyeur! Find me in the maritime
verdure (unless I see you first). I'll be at a sunrise bonfire,

coddling my perfect eggs. I won't dawdle. I'll be
the model speed-waddler off to surf a Cranberry

Oceanspray tide back to the abode where I abide me
and mine. On the bottom of my board is a warning

against mixed metaphors, and an incantation:
Whatever drives me must ease up on the throttle

because gravity is a crash-killer
and the catsup mightn't go back in the bottle.

MY LIFE IN TAXICABS

A cabbie can be a physician, a prof, a gentleman, a jerk.
A cabbie can be a magician and reduce your legwork.
In Fredericton, 1949, a cabbie was manslaughtered.
Another dead cabbie is your secret Jewish grandfather.

Taking cabs is my fulfillment of a class mobility narrative
encrypted in the dead cells of my parched arches,
buried in the marrow of my heavy metatarsals.
For catharsis, I wash the tired trotters of my *cochon*
carcass—too many marching band marches
with my *largesse*. How many Jews *does* it take to screw
in the brightest electric menorah to ever fluoresce?

A cabbie poses with his son, your father, by Halifax
Harbour. A cabbie poses proudly with his son in front
of his taxi, but then when my dad's mother remarried,
she reclaimed my dad, told him he was no longer Jewish
and would never see his father again. When the new
stepfather met his new stepson, he put down the bottle
and said, "You're fat—let's see if this stone will break
over your head." How I love and hate to repeat
myself! The allure of a cab is that someone
will come when you call and the mirage of a home
to which you can, and want to, return. A cab can take

you anywhere—to the dispensary at West Fourth and Burrard
if you want to roll one up with an onion-leaf page torn
from your unabridged work of the bard. (The professor
said it would be a good investment …).

Louis Althusser sees me on Barrington trying to hail
a cab to no avail. He doesn't turn around when I scream
Hey you! but I warned his wife that he's already set sail.
I plied him with old triangles of burning bourbon
but he said that his fate and my rhymes were altogether
overdetermined. Althusser rejected the psych ward
and killed his wife Hélène later that year, so take him
with a grain of sand in your shoe. Did it ever occur to you
that the wandering Jew just couldn't get a cab?
His corkscrew curls will sweeten the breeze 'til Easter.

He limps without rhythm. All he wants is a running metre.
What-was the-food that-fuel'd the-farts with-which this-
cab was-hot(box'd)? One hundred years ago, Halifax
exploded and the profile of a dead man still shadows
a window of St. Paul's Church on Argyle. A while ago,
it was on *Jeopardy*. What is a readymade sculpture of sham
memory? What is a salt-and-pepper portrait of a belated

> Zayde and me?   What do you call a fag
> without a cab? A hailing Mary. Is that a gaffe that
> takes us aback?   Are we afraid

of my queer linguistic bric-a-brac, the crotchety tchotchkes
of my cantankerous tongue, wrung sky-dry? In Montreal,
a glut of taxis meant my butt got cruised. They could
sniff out a fat ass in need on St. Denis, slow down until
my averted eyes signalled decline. They could sense
my tired behind, bruised cheek, on St. Zotique. They would
sneak over to the road's cold shoulder and have me
in the back seat in a busted heart's meek beat when my
smile belied a sick belly of slick smoked meat gone awry.
Some cabs stunk—goat *fromage* aged in small hay nest.

Yet I, sick wandering Jew, was often desperate for a metre.
Flus-ter'd-by mus-tard-and cuss-ing-rich cus-tard,-I'd
hop in and bastardize my address: *douze-cent* (burp)
Laurier Est? Once, on Avenue du Docteur-Penfield, a cabbie
exclaimed, "Woman drivers! Am I right? Men and women
couldn't be further apart!" "Oh, we're closer than
we seem," I said. *We* are always closer than we seem;
The call is coming from inside the house! Wouldn't it
have been just fab if I'd licked his earlobe and said,
There's a clitoris [sic] *throbbing inside of this cab!*

His wrists, my tie.   My mouth, his ascot.
Who's to say   if I did, or if I did not?

In other cabs, gratuitous diet advice: less cheese, (*cheese
makes you thick*), more cabbage, (*you're so fat I can't see
your dick*). I smell burnt bagels and flotsam floods my brain,
vexed when a cabbie calls us sisters one day and brothers
the next. I need a new necrophiliac GPS. I play chess
with Checker but they can't get me to dead grandfather
or to work. A cabbie can be a physician, a prof, a gentleman,

a jerk, a mirage, a montage, alone or a legion. Our very last
cab had a breakdown on Regent. We bought an old car
this week. I'll miss the conversations except those
in which abortion and chauvinism feature. I've always
been more afraid of a blue lagoon than a creature.

2.
TCHOTCHKES

PIONEERS

I am the first transgender person to ever take a dump wearing only a pleather hat and one psychedelic sock with a big toe sticking out of it, curling in pain at the peak of the dump, because the cat likes to chew on my socks when he's home alone but who can blame him; what would you do if you were alone all day and only ate two foods your entire life? This *holds aloft a chicken bone with lint on it* is the world's first chicken-wing bone dropped by a transgender person onto the floor while high and depressed on the couch, which was then kicked *under* the couch by a cat but then discovered by a transgender person a month later during a spell of aspiration. I am the first transgender person IN THE WORLD to fart in this seldom-used service elevator while standing on one foot rubbing my belly and tapping my head. I am the first transgender person to touch this booger and the first one to wipe it on the back of this old couch and the first one to accidentally knock it off a week later when dry and crispy and the first transgender person to roll my eyes at myself about my boogers and then include stuff about boogers in a poem. I am the first EVER transgender person in this country to drink cola (synonyms: pop; soda; soft drink; fizzy water; seltzer, etc.) while invigilating my students' exams in Masculinities class and suddenly getting my period. I am the first transgender person to snatch a dictionary off a shelf to cross out words such as *virginity, frontiers, originality, pioneers,* etc. I am the first transgender person to use "etc." in a prose poem for two *oh wait now, it's three* sentences in a row. Etc.! Etc.! Etc.!

LINES FOR A NIGHT AT THE BATHHOUSE

Coke can be ingested with a bankrupt laundry card
and spooled fiver—I saw it. I wept about him
when my host's blue budgie bird sprung loose
then returned. I saw it on the mantle, photo of a virgin
saint aspirates and cries, a faucet. *What news!*
Where is my bruise that curls like holy hair?
Probably the last place I saw it. Headless Saint
Christopher drives a hot magenta camper now,
go-goes on speakers. Chalice is empty, his tab
past due. Alone. And his god is due for an audit.

I try to get through with ambiguity while my breasts
[sic] strive to reach the slick floor. I have no dick
per se, but people aren't observant; he'd tell you
that he saw it. Condemned St. Henri co-ops can hold
dozens of freaks seeking freaks seeking the un-known
so as to own their own bones. He didn't know
he'd missed it until he saw it. Why can yeast belch
itself lighter? How far do our eruptions reach?
Could I draw it? Can gas be mapped? Do secrets smell?
Did the water lily cringe when Monet saw it?

There's no reason to push anyone anywhere
by the back of the neck. Withdrawn—coat your tone
in clover honey and just ask: why pick a bone
when you can gnaw it? The partridge in the pear tree
is lonely. The goose has no idea what's coming.
A heart bobs in a bowl of cold water in the sink
as we still try to thaw it. When I believe my eyes,
the mirage tastes like mint. I will squint 'til I see fit.
We covet touch in bubbles, and dehydrated.
Fruit, are you sure you saw all this?

RHOTACISM

- *"an excessive or idiosyncratic use of the letter R"*
- *"the inability to pronounce (or difficulty in pronouncing) R"*
- *characteristic of "Canadian Maritime English"*

The stars are hardly far.
They're just holes to darn
with yarn scarves
and bards' yarns that
quarantine quarry-hard
hearts. So don't start
with the furor of warnings
of methane barn-farts
fuelling rural Walmarts
that play the country charts.
Because smart artists
send tardy regards
to those who spat-spar
before a full overhead
compartment. We'd rather
be out in an old yard
treed with future apple tarts,
crust of lard hoarded
from hams. We Spartan
martians' kitchen party
arts sit in jars for March.
Hey! We are just our overfed
car-farts (artichoke dip).
Maybe caviar parfait
is par for your rich parts?
Makes a poor large belly barf,
eh? Rub your tummy;

rub *my* tummy. Pursue
a hardtack heart attack
over rye and cards
(gin rummy!). A sergeant's
barge on a Halifax pier
would appear marginal
if not for the warm charge
I feel in my arms
when an ocean is over.
Farmed Swiss chard
fills arms and pastoral art.
But if we are tartan-garbed,
we are plaid birds
on barbed wire. Were we
poor? And are we rebuilding
buildings we set on fire?

YOU ARE INTRUDER MOUSE

I'm gayer than the lesbian scene of *Being Erica* is straight.
I'm the Ursula to your Phoebe, friend. Jessica to your Sweet
Valley Elizabeth. You are Tongue-Twister; I am Shibboleth.
I'm the syphilitic portion of Nietzsche's life wrung dry.
I'm the doctor that depresses your tongue, but why am I

a beauty burden wrapped up in ugly fruit? I'm the pith
you spit with pity, my unpretty; to my Beer, you are the Root.
To my Seven-, you are -Up. I Am Sippy! YOU ARE CUP!
I'm a narcissist squinting into fizz and these bubbles
make me think I have a fly's eyes. I sigh when I must try

to shyly disguise my thigh's gaping holes. I grew up
near mountains that were incestuous molehills.
At eighteen I was certain I too would die. I was addicted
to my spit-shine sigh. I was the errant splash of purple
that homogenized your tie-dyed meandering shoes.

I'm a photo still of you: windowsill with shoofly pie.
You are Bake; none are Broil; I am Deep Fry. You are Oil.
You are Water. I AM EMULSIFY. I watch lumberjacks
carve softwood like margarine that has not been dyed
yellow due to the strength of the dairy lobby in Quebec.

"Friends" think it's déclassé and lazy to take taxis
but have strong opinions about Uber and What! Marx!
Would! Do! You are to Marx what an ant was to Engels; I am
to the Bangles what simile is to ♫ *walk like an* ♫
encryption. I wish for my cells to need only a meagre,

only a fun, prescription. I'm an advertisement. There is no
product. You're a draft of a jingle that came to Don Draper
mid-orgasm in a redacted bathhouse scene. His suit
is a full-metal jacket. I am Joker and he is a queen.
I'm Peggy to your Don; you're Betty to my Glen. I'm the un-

broken bottle of Canadian Club in your burnt-down pub.
You're Charlie to Snoopy, but I'm dust to Pigpen. I'm the cat
and I'm the fleas. The blue vein *and* the cheese.
I am Down to your Kicking Me, I am Lips to the Man
Without a Face. You are Intruder Mouse. I am CRAWLSPACE.

THE MIDNIGHT LUNCH WHISTLE BLOWS AT
THE HOLY COMMUNION FACTORY

Sister Mary Iris, a former nun-*cum*-outcast, came one time too many within the convent walls, was excommunicated and became the night manager of the wafer line at Human Communion Incorporated where she watches machines punch crisp panels of wafer into tiny would-be Christ bites.

The delivery dude flicks some lint off his grey corduroy pants, tries to look debonair leaning on the wall, and asks Mary Iris to *scribble her Jane Han... cock* on the form for he's just placed a box of flour at her feet. After surveying her cropped, russet-grey coif, he almost writes her off when he notices the tapered pants that must reach her areolas. (Has he seen her before? At a womyn-space dance, maybe?) The phrase "wardrobe malfunction" ought to have been reserved for such fashion anarchy, though perhaps *fashion agnosticism* is more the phrase. Mary Iris's right hand is already thrust deep enough into her pocket to make strangers with children suspicious, but it's only her fifth month in civvies and, while pockets are no baggy habit, they're her only cover. When asked for her signature, she jams her hand in further, starts to sweat and wonders if her attempts to become ambidextrous have been successful.

Harold, the regular delivery man, knows all about Mary Iris's accident and the way she prefers him to look away as she signs the form with the four and a half fingers on her right hand. Harold also makes his deliveries during the daytime like a regular adult. But this fellow (she thinks it's a fellow but those mellow hazel eyes, honeyed hair, that pair of breasts—or are they pecs?—confuse her, and how did he get that bruise on his fleecy neck?) knows nothing and tries to small-talk: *Bread as far as the eye can see and not a bite to eat, eh?* (It is an affront to "Truth" that Christians call this "bread," this matter so dry it once pasted itself to Mary Iris's tonsils for the entire closing prayer until she ran to the back seat of her old Chevette to soak Jesus off with holy water.)

Uh, ha ha... yeah. She laughs like kids do when their parents are in the room and a sex scene comes on TV, takes out her hands, strips them of the latex gloves the workers all wear, and, groping the air for the pen, drops it. *Let me grab that for you,* the delivery guy says, swaggering over and kneeling. Sister Mary Iris wonders if he is one of those people she has seen on *Oprah.* There were no televisions in the convent, but the break room at Human Communion Incorporated has a small black-and-white set. Yes, she thinks, perhaps he is one of those curiouser youth who transubstantiate flesh. The need for politesse ruptures her wonderings and she replies humbly, *Thanks.* Down there, he's inches from her interrupted finger.

On her first day as shift manager, there was an accident. The wafer line starts with a cluster of sharp circular moulds that descend like a guillotine upon the wafer, leaving in its floury wake four hundred more-or-less perfect hosts and rubbish edges. But that day, Mary Iris was thinking too much about her likely lapsed garden at St. Martha's. (Sister Mary Laura had been chosen as the new keeper of the convent's plot, and Mary Iris rolled her eyes skyward—to whom, we are not sure—when she imagined what Mary Laura's brown thumbs would do to her former Eden.) Moving at that viscous speed of nostalgia, she didn't digest what had happened until, in the place of the 399th host, sat an inch of knuckle, cuticle and sub-nail grime. By the time she looked up, half her finger sat in the "seconds" bin destined for Protestant churches. She wrapped her gushing nub in one-ply toilet paper, said, *I'm not feeling so well. See you all tomorrow,* and soon was, by the grace of God, tied up by doctors in a whole maze of gauze. And here we thought Jesus hated disability.

Mary Iris sees the delivery fellow looking, with curiosity, at her hand. Instead of relaying the real tale, Mary Iris tells him, noting that his name badge must have been torn off with teeth, *Ahh, the trunk of my car, umm, you know... I'm careless...*

Does it, like, freak out your co-workers? ...And are they cool with you being, umm, you know a—

Before he can say "dyke," Sister Mary Iris innocently cuts him off: *an amputee?*

(Her colleagues think her courageous, but they look at her finger as if the scars were bastard stigmata. They hide from her by requesting special assignments in the quality management department, flanking the conveyor belt to flip the oblong, octagonal or otherwise deformed hosts off the belt with a knife made specially for this purpose by 3M, into a box that will be triple-taped and sent to NASA to be pressed, chipboard-style, into pieces of astronaut bread to be consumed in some other upside-down world.)

Hmmm, does it bother *them? I don't think so, I mean, it takes some getting used to I'm sure.*

Maybe he *hasn't* seen her before. Maybe she's not an old queer after all. He tries one last time. *Does it bother you? If you don't mind me asking.*

A month after the accident, she finally stopped stuffing the glove finger with an inch of Kleenex at the end like an anxious young woman might once have done with a training bra. *Umm*, she ventures, *I don't really think about it much, so... ummm... not really.*

As they try to figure out who has to speak next, they would both like to undo this conversation (which has been spoken in that churchy tone that turns every word inside out: peace-be-with-you-and-also-with-you). The delivery person is still kneeling on the floor grasping the pen. As they realize this, they both hustle to defeat this impasse of bodily follies. In his haste to stand, he steps on her toe, and falls back to his knee. When her limbs go akimbo out of pain and imbalance, her right hand strikes his face. She's so mortified by the human contact that she could vomit. Instead, she ejaculates, *Jesus! I'm so sorry, I'm so, so—*

But he's not mad. He is not risen and he is not moving. He still feels her half-finger on his face. It's the first time that someone (not in a white coat) has touched the new digit. She lets both fists unravel and extends her right hand again in cryptic blessing and material apology.

He moves closer like someone about to complete a drug deal. *So are you... you know... a "sister?"*

Surely this lingo will speak to her! His gaydar hums like the first pocket-rocket he bought when he was a fourteen-year-old with a training bra. Mary Iris is stunned that she still looks the part of a nun. *Yes*, she affirms, *is it that obvious?* He replies, *Umm, yeah. And I'm never wrong.*

Sister Mary Iris wonders why this punk has such strong feelings about being able to identify a nun by looking at her. Before she can figure out the subtext, his next movement takes her aback. He leans forward as though beckoned by the small finger, rubs his face against it like a cat, and kisses it like Judas did Jesus. Mary Iris nods and moves her wrist against her pelvis. He takes her short finger into his mouth and slowly moves his head. In some unorganized upwelling of affect, Sister Mary Iris grasps the door frame of the lunchroom with her left hand and puts one foot atop the box of unholy, whole-wheat flour that will soon be made flesh and swallowed. Somewhere between shrunken-Catholic-finger and circumcised-Jewish-phantom, her little limb only measures half an inch square. But, they both feel it over and under their clothes when her foot slips from the box to the floor, her hand latches to the side of his head, and the machines all shut down because the midnight lunch whistle blows.

DUDEBRO POETRY

Dudebro poetry pretends to forget your name.
Dudebro poetry can't act for shit.

Dudebro poetry wears plaid while reading a poem
that complains about women who wear plaid.

Dudebro poetry thinks it is the new lemon gin.
Dudebro poetry is the new warm beer.

Dudebro poetry is written by people
who don't like the passive voice.

Dudebro poetry has your best interest at heart.
Dudebro poetry encourages you to self-publish.

Dudebro poetry jokes about Frida Kahlo's vagina.
Dudebro poetry arrives after the other authors have read.

Dudebro poetry says poetry is useless at times of political
crisis. Dudebro poetry can't even volunteer at a food bank.

Dudebro poetry will never run out of metaphors
for the small of a woman's back or her smile.

Dudebro poetry asks you to call him
when someone posts relevant info to the listserv.

Dudebro poetry is a light bulb, thin cardboard sleeve,
a blacklight bowling party with your church group.

Dudebro poetry can't wait to grieve deeply.
Dudebro poetry can't even approach the melancholic.

Dudebro poetry will not give up its seat on the bus.
Dudebro poetry thinks that being sensitive is an alibi.

Dudebro poetry thinks it is the exception. It is the rule.
Dudebro poetry thinks that list poems are lazy.

101 INTERPELLATIONS ON NINETY-NINTH AVENUE

(Statements Uttered to Me by Strangers on Edmonton Sidewalks)

You sellin'? You buyin'? I thought you were tryin'
to cruise me, dude! Got any change man? Got any change
ma'am? Well, it looks like you do! I'll take an IOU. You … you …

Excuse me, um, I need to go to Clareview—
do you know where the nearest LSD station is?[1]

Dude, you gotta lose some weight … like, I can't even see
your dick. Dude, that don't sound right. Your voice
don't sound right. Dude, I wouldn't wear that pink tie
in this neighbourhood if I were you … you … you …

You are so handsome. Do you wanna smoke a J
and just see what happens? With some people it's difficult
to tell whether they are man or woman and you are
one of those people. You need a woman to carry
those groceries for you. God bless you … you …

Where to, big guy, chief, sport, pal, champ? If I don't
see you again down here, I'll see you up there, girl.
That's quite a haircut you got there. You better run fast,
bitch, you … You are a lucky man, my friend. You are.

---

1   Edmonton's subway system is called the LRT (Light Rail Transit).

Are you... a lesbian? WOOOO! Dude, that's a lesbian!
Do us a favour and make out! Wow, I can't believe you all use
[   ] as a man's name out east! Lucas? Well, I gotta
tell ya, you look more like a Lucy. How much do you weigh?
You don't know anything—all YOU care about is FOOD!

Fag or dyke?
FAG OR DYKE?!
What the fuck are you?
You... you... you...?

IT'S LIKE WE HAVE ESPN OR SOMETHING

The aquarium cancelled the Valentine's Day
"Octopus Mating Event" due to cannibalism concerns.
But I want you and I to eat each other's sounds
until we die of whimsy, then frenzy, then dysentery.
We don't need sixteen arms with our feral
senses, see?

My uncle (he is my cousin but I barnacle to youth)
wants me to try ayahuasca with his seashore shaman.
But I want you and I to swallow all our grafts,
fit our survival tools with concrete feet, stone-skip
them across surf. In your language, they call this [   ].
In my grandfather's Russian, it's pancakes
(well, blini).

We have used that far-feeling telepathy to design
our tag-team to-do list: first, blitzkrieg all lists; shame
sham taxonomies; misalign your ribs; put an apple
in my mouth and fingernail-score my skin,
crackling darling. Let us be the spoiled creamers
that curdle their commutes.

Let us become the unchained melody, rechained.
Don't be afraid. Or do, then roll yourself in the smoke
and sawdust and spilt oil of you and whoever
you resemble, or try (not) to.

WHERE THE HEART ISN'T

Home is where the heart *isn't*—where the heart goes missing.
It trots off, syncopated, in a left-footed waltz, spinning, guiding
your feet into too-tight shoes, unswayed, unstretched by you.

Home is where the heart *isn't*—where it is too coincident
with the sedimentation of chipped wallpapers. There's no linen,
lace or currency tender enough to earn your hard heart
a proper place-card at the adult dinner table.

Home is where your jizz jets, piss tinkles, spit fizzes,
where Ma rules and Pop rocks or where someone closes doors
and someone's always gone. Where Mom and Dad threw away
the combination to a vault you've forgotten like a lost gym lock.

Home is where your arteries twinge, where your toxic cocktail
of C*tholic Conscience and C*ltic Soul binges. Purgatory
may hurt but at least *there* everyone is heading elsewhere.

Hearts are a wrecking ball, a huff-puff runaround. Houses
are bound by foundations, are sticks and stones glued down.

So tighten your belt. Or. Just. Buckle.

A heartbeat, in the end, is a countdown: x number of years
out west, too many mojitos and maybe, home-stretching,
you'll have won. How does one engrave the right to jump,

to restart? Just walk away with a framed, failed
echocardiogram chart, marching with the cadence
of your *lub-dub* limp set to the drum of your hat-stand heart.

NO, DADDY, NO

I.

I just joined a fraternity for bratty boys. A brat-ernity.
We eat cream pi, share rooms at the Delta,
are anything but alpha. Bet you might want to join!

Our skin is so thick that we don't need leather. (Regardless,
the rest are vegan and make their whips out of old bike tires:
Reuse; Recycle; Recline on this here air mattress, my friend.)

Someone fucked one of them in front of the others
in a condemned house in St. Henri. In the middle,
one screamed, "No, daddy, no!" And if you think

sex can't be a salve, just leave your membership card
and key fob. Did someone slap me so hard I began
to sob? If so, I'm part of the pack now,

but they have yet to show me the group's secret hand job.
Oh, get a grip. Don't be on edge.
Here's what one does to pledge!

You sit in the lap of Sylvia Plath, suck off her
pretty red strap-on and slide it up 'til it really hurts.
(And all I get is this lousy T-shirt? A pain in the ass,

a massive piercing through my fat white heart
and a small part in George Michael's next video?)
Be half a dyke, half a fag, all limp and no swagger.

Be a colourful character with no faith in dull Hughes.
Not all slaps and bruises are alike.
Read a pained body like a canvas.

II.

"No, Daddy, No!" These are words that polite houseguests
avoid or explain. You're so vain, Dr. Freud, I'm sure you think
this poem is about you.

You're 25 percent right, despite your incitement
to intercourse and of course your indictment of we queers
who you may believe want to fuck our mommies.

Freud 101: Dreams, Dicks and Daddies... for Dummies.
This stanza *is* about you, about how easy it is
to doubt you before your actual oeuvre has outed you

as paying heed to one thousand other things, such as
millipedes, which you configured as kind of trans and
sort of gay. But that work didn't really have legs, eh?

(I know, I know. I'd do anything for a pun and it shows,
even sail to France with Jacques Lacan on a fleet
of a thousand bateaus to show those in the know that taking

back a lack
of anything
can be hot.)

The point is this:
I've got a new
antidote.

It involves a ball gag and not a few toys.
I call it the silent cure and you can't
talk your way out of it, boy.

Do you remember Freud's case history, "Fragments of
an Analysis of a Case of Hysteria: The Case of Dora"?
That explorer that Freud thought was a liar (liar),

she dreamt her house was on fire and her father was standing
next to her bed. In her next dream, Dad was dead and she
couldn't roam her way home in time. Is that how it goes?

Or did she see him a few days before, held together by strong
staples that would shut up anyone, evermore? Staples of
higher quality than the thread they thread through

fathers' lips when they're dead. Isn't it fun
when poets bring up personal loss for street cred?
Plath thinks it's just a gas.

III.

I joined a fraternity. We have bunkbeds and nicknames
and everything. They call me [   ] and crawl
toward someone at night to be nursed. Old boys get thirsty.

Like you, they all have their own disgusting way of feeling
taken care of. Love sure isn't the only method of assimilating
your past into a way you want to be felt and feel.

Never fear, there's no queer Oedipus here. My primal scene
is replayed on the "screen memories" of TV. Offstage sex
that binds people together. All the wrong kinds of bondage.

So which is your fetish? Manacles? Mortgages? Cars?
Back seats? Wanna pickup truck? Death drive,
perhaps while blotto? Dora's daddy was named Otto.

So was Plath's. Sorry, we're fresh
out of jokes today. Just piss play
or whore d'oeuvres? I'd love to!

Which investments
do you own—
up to?

PARK LANE

A head can be an old Body Shop.
A body can be an old head shop.

Your Satsuma sneeze makes me gag
each time. I'm weed-weak

in the kneeling pulse of my fag-
niche prime. The plywood

of your skull leaks Oceania oil
but you never moved with a current.

We were ripened patchouli sweaters
sopping up spilt swill of white musk.

YOU straightened out like corn.
You mistook ME for your husk.

But I'm in cyan silk and will not
attend your crop. Your head

is a boarded-up Body Shop.
My body is not an old head shop

but there were short dank years
of candy-crushed phones and unlucky

coins that I wouldn't scrub
with strawberry soap for new bones

or new joints. Did you ever have
a bilingual gay lap dance to a Cranberries

ballad? Break your finger at a party
in a condemned house filled

with dumpster clementines? Do you know
how to vanish? Why Montreal is a verb?

Are you still perturbed if a friend
comes up queer? Oh, Ph.D. You never

could see me. In your sterile-soap
dystopia of white things, I'd slow-gait

evaporate—smoke rings, fat sweat.
I walk by Lush on Robson and surrender

my nostrils to its floral flatulence.
There's a TWO-FOR-ONE BATH 💣 sale,

but where's my FREE BODY BUTTER
FOR ALL SELF-FLAGELLANTS?

I WANT A PRIME MINISTER WHO CRIES

after Zoe Leonard

Sure, I want a prime minister who cries
when Gord Downie dies. I want a prime minister
who was listening to Lido Pimienta before she was cool.
I want a prime minister who *fermes* his *gueule*
and lets his backbone slide. I want a prime minister
who cried when Aaliyah died even though
she was American. I want a prime minister
who believes that age is just a number.
I want a prime minister who cries for René Angélil.
I want a prime minister who wonders if it's too late
now to say sorry. I want a prime minister who knows
that apologies are only a beginning. I want a prime minister
whose guilty feet have got no rhythm, who has faith-a-faith
in the busted beat of a broken metronome. I want
a prime minister who is tired of being touched
by strangers on the metro. I want a prime minister
who recites the "I Want a President" poem Zoe Leonard
wrote and I want a prime minister who cries
when Celine hits the high note.

Sure, I want a prime minister who admits to smoking
weed. I need a prime minister who was a sandwich artist,
who toasted your sub while baked. I want a prime minister
who quit Narcotics Anonymous because there were
too many homophobes. I want a prime minister with fetal
alcohol syndrome. I want a fat prime minister, and soon.
I want a teen-wolf prime minister who changes
gender every full, every half, every harvest moon.
I want a prime minister who cooks junk and eats cake batter

with the same singed spoon. I want a prime minister
who burned my village to the ground. I want a prime minister
whose campaign HQ was a supervised injection site.
I want a prime minister with type two diabetes
and stage four lung cancer. I want a prime minister
who celebrates the sesquicentennial spectacle by sinking
a stake into the heart of fentanyl. I want a prime minister
with poor parents and who giggles when she mispronounces
Oed-i-pal after too strong an ed-ib-le. I want an electric
prime minister who sees all the energy it takes
to get through a day. I want a prime minister who cries
for the dead busker who couldn't even play.

Sure, I want a prime minister with funky socks.
I want a prime minister who gets your rocks off for cash.
I want a prime minister who coaxes me with a northern touch.
I want a prime minister who wears a red shawl.
I want a prime minister who knows that he doesn't know it all,
who listens to us. I want a prime minister who wears her niqab
on the #80 Avenue de Parc autobus. I want a prime minister
who knows that no settlement is enough.
I want a prime minister whose last breath was taken
on the *Komagata Maru* or another vessel we sent back to death.
I want a prime minister who would meet me at the S.S. *St. Louis*
and not bail. (I want a prime minister who knows
this ship has sailed!) I want a prime minister whose great-
grandfather was a fourth-class passenger who ended up
in NS instead of NYC. I want a prime minister who's a broken
man on a Halifax pier. I want a prime minister who drives
through "the bad 'hood" and doesn't reach for the locks.
I want a prime minister with blood-crusted, rain-rusted socks.

Sure, I want a prime minister who goes to the pride parade.
I want a prime minister who quit the pride board
when it went corporate. I want a prison abolitionist
for prime minister. I want a prime minister whose Canadian
tuxedo includes leather and a harness. Yes, I want
a submissive prime minister, a prime minister
who started at the bottom (now she's here),
who has pushed the limits of the body in a manner other
than hiking or jogging. I want a prime minister
who is queerer than a two-dollar bill, who is thirty-eight
years old and never kissed a girl. I want a prime minister
on PrEP, or not. I want a prime minister who has AIDS.
I want a prime minister with hot flashes or night terrors.
I want a prime minister who is bad at sex, fumbling toward
debauchery. I want a prime minister who will hold me down
and kiss me so hard, who takes my breath away. I want
a prime minister who eats peaches and fucks the pain away.

I want a prime minister who cries
when Gord Downie dies and when Indigenous kids kill
themselves or drink the waters we've muddied.
I want a prime minister who has buried hearts at Oka, who
grew up east of the hundredth meridian. I want a prime minister
who does not excuse abuse. I want a prime minister
who is a queer instead of an ally, a patient instead of a doctor,
the criminal not the cop, the slut not the shamer,
nor a settler for whom we settle. I want a prime minister
who doesn't love power. I'm not sure I want a prime minister.
Do we need another hero? Is that all there is?
I want a prime minister who oughta know.
I want a prime minister who knows what the poets are doing.

WORKING TITLES FOR GUY FIERI'S *DINERS, DRIVE-INS AND DIVES*

Abattoirs, Abortuaries and America (HOO-RAH)

Bleach and Beer-Batters, Batman!

Camaro… Catchphrases… Catachresis…

Donkey-sauce; Donkey-sauce; Donkey-sauce

Ed (Hardy) / Edibles (Hearty)

Food-Lube and Folksy Flatulence in Flavortown

Go Big; Go Home; Goatee

Holy-Moly-Stromboli, How Have I Watched Three Hours of This?

"I can't go on, I'll go on"

Jagged Little Swill

Kid Rock's Bromantic Variety Show

Les Liasons Dangereuses de Lukewarm Leftovers, Listeria
  and Lavatories

Motley Cue™ Mansplainer and His Band the Hollandaise Malaise

Not Unless You've Lost the Remote Control

On the Road, Part Two: Outta-Bounds 'n' Off-the-Hook

Patriotic Pieholes and Postprandial Pain

~~Quinoa~~

Rockabilly Reruns ♫ on Route 66 ♫

SUPERCALIFRAGILISTICEXPIALIDOCIOUS

The Horror! The challah!

Ubiquity, Umbrage and Unguents

Velveeta, Vasectomies and Valour

Wraparounds!

XTRA XTREME EGGZ BENEDICT

Y. No Really. WHY. Twenty-four Seasons.

Zzzzzzzzz

3.
CRAZY IN LOVE

SEPARATION

I would root for every underdog
to rise to the occasion of you.

I would root like an ossified Expos fan
but you gotta call 'em as you sees 'em,

and sometimes the called third
is obvious enough to hurt on replay.

The inside corner is an intimate
flirtation. Somebody is always out.

Don't balk. Bunting is overrated,
men. Sacrifice doesn't fly.

Bury the golden gloves. Lay down
your devilled defences to swing

for the land of no fences. Ignore
the green monster. To mix sports

metaphors in my fey way, I'll skate
from York to Queen. Please don't

Nancy Kerrigan me. Please keep caring
about my sorrow-sore knees and me.

Whatever the score, I'd still say, *Hey, hey,*
you're okay. I would still want to lift you

up, up, up and away.

VISION

If I wore my partners' glasses, would I see things differently?
(Yes, students: worlds hinge on the placement of an apostrophe.)

If I retrieved my partner's glasses from a sadist sea,
what would I hear during such a deep dive?

Sometimes I think I need a spot of silence. Even the seabed
of the Mariana Trench is lousy with earthquake clamour.

If I wore my partners' glasses, would you feel my polyphonic
grammar? Would you hate me? After all, everyone

is a poor nail if you're just a
sledgehammer. Are you a tool?

Glaciers are melting, scientists say. Ocean floors sink due
to extra weight. I am heavy. When I'm a ready river, don't be

the levee. If virtue springs from going with the flow, condemn
me. Justice impairs all our body parts. Bethany the waitress

eyes me and what she sees is that you're twenty thousand
leagues out of my league (we may disagree).

On television, someone leaves; someone strays; someone
stays. Simple Simon says that you can never have it both ways.

I want to say we can, but bifocals are not covered by
the company health plan. We are all eclipsed,

burnt-out retinas. We all have cataracts.

This is not metaphor. I need contact. I need contacts.

THESES ON THE HYDROLOGY OF SWEET TEA

Steep me like tea in a scalding sea.
Pour the brew on the roots of a tree.

Look up, up for brush
when you worry. It's me.

Follow my coniferous coif home,
but cut me down if need be. Chopping

spree. Decisions are arduous; love
can be trigonometry. All straight lines

can be expressed as $y=mx+b$,
but we are not formulaic, you see?

We leave Points A and B
to the petite bourgeoisie, to rampart

hearts that beat, badly, in barracks
under lock and lost skeleton

key. Sweet tea, when you need a hand,
grasp my trunk tightly.

Call that synecdoche. Call it "come
sit next to me." Call it:

I know you'd undrape the nape
of your neck for me, would unwind

the twine and silver filigree
that stitch your scar tissue into Body,

into your Möbius-stripped-down
topology. Climb on top of me. Open.

Let's oxidize our insides out,
if we have such sacred architectures.

I pray only to wordplay. Am I wrong
to fetishize fluidity? Strength? To steep

your oolong too, too long? A chemist-
chef has concocted a double-edged tea:

a drink that is half hot, half cold.
To which side of the cup

would an optimist first lend her lips?
You and I wouldn't choose; we'd sip

from both parts at once. My partner
gave me the chemist-chef's cookbook.

Your ex gave you many of your favourite
teapots. Dr. Phil would ask

what in tarnation we think we're doing.
In his experience, too many chefs

means there's trouble brewing.
But what is excess? What is shame?

Is it hot and cold kissing? Is it the kettle
wet-hissing your name? The secret

of the queer tea: the cup is filled
with a liquid gel divided into two

temperatures, so that the potion's
imperceptible viscosity prevents mixing.

Just a gel, for all that fuss, just a semi-
solid masquerading as fluid, as us.

R_X

To my new lover's lover, my new lover's love
for me is a case of Wanting Too Much
(with features of Generalized Disorder Disorder).

At her chest, my ears hear her synaesthete mystery.
Reciprocally, I offer a taste of my own doctored
history: massage therapist says the deep

small of my back disagrees with me.
Québécois chiropractor says my knee jerks
with a dummy's hyper-mobility.

My skin is too thick. I bleed like a weed.
Turns out the therapist sees both my new lover
and me. This is college-town sociology,

our pastoral phantasmagoria. My gender may engender
all my practitioners' dysphoria. Why do minds
attic-stack themselves with empty frames?

It's enough clutter to undo a hoarder. After all is said
and so little done, the Pursuit of the Normal is just
Avoidance Disorder. My new lover says my incisors incite

geysers, but in truth, I'm too long in the tooth
for this. Such rhymes aren't spry. But I try
to syllabus-stress myself back into feeling smart.

This is just one symptom of an enlarged heart.
She thinks I'm sweet. My opinion
is that she's just so fucking easy to treat.

POTENTIAL STOPS ON OUR MARITIME BOOK TOUR

Let us pack our matching baggage!

In Sackville, WWII radio towers transmitted
frequencies well into our millennium. Residents
heard voices haunting their Sunday night sinks
until the towers tumbled. Don't bother
wringing your dishpan hands—whet axes
and dry herbs for the artisan empire.

Pregnancy tests carpet the Dieppe mall bathroom.
To expulse or not to expulse. Evangeline,
did you go to the appointment alone?

In Antigonish, bishops move obliquely.
Check blind spots for crooked spooks, for
shadow popes on ropes, for a pilgrim girl [sic]
who doesn't know she's a Jew.

Everywhere, you and I skip Mass
to try weightlessness.

In Sydney, I miss my fellow phantom faggots
who would cruise the fruit loop for ass.
In Sydney, echo; recurrence. Biscuits
with jam, clotted dreams and molasses.

We gab but there's a sonnet corona
in your whimper. We are old oaks in thunder.
We are trust falls timbered, sweet tree, sweet tea.

Halifax?
O Memory.

In our Fredericton downtown, two dumpsters
face off. One reads, GO FOR IT. The other, SAFETY FIRST.

Look left to right to left. Tie up mixed messages
in thin leather laces. Try not to know what to do.

Just let me be gorgeous trash, here,
and there, and there, with you.

NOURISH

Our dead parents food-shame each other
in an after world insulated with bricks of devil's food
cake, mortared with pestilence.

Mortify your own flesh, martyrs without a cause.
Whip some sick cream. Get it while it's fresh.

Deals with demons don't come for free. An apple
a day doesn't fall far from the tree.

The string-bean wish of the mother stings.
The sin of the father knows best.

We set burnt maple tables with guilt-green linen
at their behest. I picture them playing chess

with carved-carrot pawns for a prize of raw prawn
on burnt bread. A toast to the chef! And to his full

retinue who have prepared this tasting
(of-your-own-medicine) menu:

- MICROWAVED TURKEY
  ROTTING IN A GARAGE
- A BARRAGE OF PEPPERONI,
  DEEP-FRIED IN SHALLOW SHAME
- ASPARTAMED YOGURT
- WILD GAME GONE RANCID
  WITH FARMER'S MARBLE SLICES.
- PIE SPICES ON THE STOVE
  MULLING OVER JUST NOTHING.

- A MODEL OF A POUND OF FLESH
  ON THE DESK AT DIET CENTRE
  USED AS A PAPERWEIGHT.

Wait—

What can we eat instead?

Gnaw on neck hairs. Pair low-hanging fruit
with high stakes. Shake and break

my will in two, into too many goosebumps.
Eat gooseberries, eat choked-up chokecherries.

How many people are on diets the day they die?
Will St. Michael catch their good sides?

At the gates, I am fat Vitruvian man—symmetrical
chins and nutcracking quads akimbo.

Befores and afters
make life just limbo.

So we straddle eras to oar
away in a blue canoe,

laugh at the two loons
gliding down the river

with the stupid settler name. Eat.
Paddle away through familial white flame.

ESSENTIAL OILS AND PRECIOUS METALS

I bellowed your name underwater in the Atlantic.
If only 75 percent of the Earth's surface ripples
with my call, is that enough undulation to move you
in three-quarter time? Waltz to me, good girl,
                              and I'll buoy you to boyhood.

Economy of language means we write candy floss and then
distill it to diamonds. But I like my sweet things to melt
on the tongue. I take my love aerated, diffuse, double-spaced.

On my lap, you melted. I wrung out my pants,
funnelled your fluid into a copper bottle, marked it *Laughing Gas*
and stowed it in my apothecary table between *Laudanum*
and *Lavender*. But we are both less essence than effervescence.

I massage peppermint and eucalyptus oil into your temples
as if fingering a future from a crystal ball. Don't fuck
     with *my gypsy ancestress and my weird luck*
     and my tarot pack and my tarot pack.
Just call me, maybe, a crackerjack megalomaniac.
Don't forget me on your travels. Woe is thee, amnesiac!

You are my iron supplement who passes me her period.
When I leave, a lip-split schlock, I spit blood like a cross-checker
off to the box. For just two minutes, we seize time.
                              Our freak-sleek equinox.

In unique New York, an elevated train track holds
my old poems and a gem or two for you. Let's bite lips
on its platinum paths, shred our passports, chip away
at your rose quartz armour, mon amour.

Rumpelstiltskin, what can I say? We spun a weekend
into gold with not even one roll into hay. You get a medal
for not saying my natal name. We don't meddle with
the fatal shame of waiting games. Now, can we play?

Can we fall on our knees to mine each
other, sleep-deep with musky need?

      This is a please this is a please.

CASSIDY

Pet me like your dead dog, your shaved-cat
smooth skin on my grizzled hide;
make manifest the pack instinct that throbs
in the seersucker air between our mouths.
It dries the matching scratch marks that score us.
My hashtagged back renders fat in heat.
The clean crumbs of what didn't have to fall
from the table are all we colicky need to eat
but water me with lion-hearted nipples
and I won't packrat our receipts. Pet me
like your dead dog named like me
and we'll see how to speak bespoke words
in ripped stitches; how to wear me; how to use
my fetching bones to sick-stroke your stale grief.

QUEER CONDITIONS FOR THRIVING

If one rotten apple spoils the family tree,
If Eve's weight was never watched by a mother,
If the past participle of "to writhe" ought to be "just shudder,"
If I can never eat you with the father tongue I can't reach,
If my fits of pique bespeak not bad behaviour but restless lesion,
If December is doubtless scar-tissue season,
If final exams are origin stories,
If the quizzes say you're Rachel and I'm Ross,
If we were on a Breakdown Express with no double berths,
If the self you might have been just got the skill-testing question wrong,
If, in cold ears, damp breath insists, *Don't stop don't stop okay,*
If, in warm years, new islands punctuate the dying sea each day,
If the red cider is spiked with the brackish bloodlust of slut saints,
If they ascertain we are oil-water, rough-lustrous, then what?

SEPARATION (2)

All the drag kings' horses
and all the trans men

can't put a good egg
or a man back together again.

It won't all come out in the wash.
Red dye is thicker than warm water.

Delicates and wools are antagonists.
This does not make me sort anything out.

The underwire bursts free from the bra.
Or is that shrapnel the bone of a whale?

The lint trap is camel-wool full.
DRIP-DRY DRIP-DRY DRIP-DRY

to no avail. All the failed genders
and all my King Street friends

know how to survive
being put through the ringer

and don't want to live with
the tyranny of a whole human again.

Pull a long hair from my sweater
and hold it as you might a kite line

or a pull-string that could make them all
say just what you want to hear.

NOUNS THAT FAIL TO CAPTURE IT

Movable feasts
(warm hummus and cheese).

Feral beasts.
Creatures.

Clandestine quarterbacks
under the bleachers.

Broken back slung up
in junky traction.

Feature Presentation; Coming
Attraction. Animal magnetic poetry.

Fictive fractals rendered
in dirty-digit dactyls.

Gentle gentile and belated
Jew at a secular Seder.

Drug-free highest
common denominator.

Never bored.
Never phony.

Lovely Us in the Psych Ward.
(You can have my macaroni.)

Blue-bruised oafs. Scabbed skins.
Gumdrop loaves. Remixed hymns

to hum off-key
as we swim.

Corkscrewed
phantom limbs.

FOURTEEN WAYS WE COULD FAIL AT BDSM

Tie you up with silly string. Let it melt.
Whip me with a fan belt and expect me to rev.
Overemphasis on techne; much fuss, much muss.
Truss you like a turkey. (You're vegetarian.)
Tell you I'm supposebly a top. (You're also a grammarian.)
Tell me you don't even like kissing before our lips
have bled. Stop wandering when we've finally nailed down
a second-best bed. Cut up our respective DSM entries
into sexual prompts and draw from a hat—wait,
that might be hot. Dada. Forget that traumas
transmogrify suddenly—crack of an invisible whip.
Forget that a mother can father-figure a flagrant fag.
Dishwash the imaginary plastic purple ball gag.
Let *it* melt. Sound off like greedy babies denied
the long lovely latch. Strike us not against
a brick wall. Forget that's how we match.

DAIRY

Colostrum, the risen cream that feeds a baby
first. If you save some for me,

we'll continue to cream our jeans like nineties teens.
You memorialize your pregnancy tits,

their sway. Let me boil your milk gently
then spoil it with citrus to split

your curds from your whey. Let me weigh you down.
Press me into and out of shape.

Age me. Brine you. Grill me. Tuck you
into a buckwheat crepe. Would I eat you

from a lukewarm baggie on a Couche-Tard counter
on Sherbrooke? WHY NOT! WHAT THE HELL!

You say fucking that day was like being
the butter that becomes my salted caramel.

CONJUNCTION TUTORIAL

We know what "depression clothes" means because
we've worn them all before, but, we kept brand-new
black hoodies and black dresses on hand (respectively)
SO THAT one day, IN THE EVENT THAT we felt better,
we could wear them, both for pleasure AND pride,
AS MUCH as for comfort. YET, there's a new shade of black,
FOR science has discovered a way to shed less light, EVEN
IF illumination remains all the rage, NOT ONLY because
we are afraid of the dark, BUT, also, because we do not
understand our depths UNTIL we are out of them.
You mustn't EITHER wear a summer dress of this
black LEST I fall into it AS SOON AS I see you, ALTHOUGH
it is a moot point, FOR the shade—Vantablack—
is highly inaccessible, EVEN THOUGH one might assume
that colours are democratic, BUT pigment is always
political, SO, one artist now owns all rights to paint
with the blackest black, AS IF that makes him deep,
NOW THAT he is the only one who can legally smear
a shade that deflects 99.96 percent of light, reflecting
NEITHER that from the sun NOR from a flicked Bic,
NEITHER that from the moon NOR from the spark of the
flint that the cadet strikes against steel in the woods.
WHETHER it's because we drift through each other
without gravity or because metaphors of colour tend
to be problematic, AS SOON AS I heard of Vantablack
and its refusal to refract light, AS SOON AS I saw you
in your sleeveless black sundress, I thought about
depression clothes. I thought about so many people
from our pasts, our own failures. Then I realized
the extent to which people go in order to not reflect.
Then I called you. Then I put on my pink party suit.

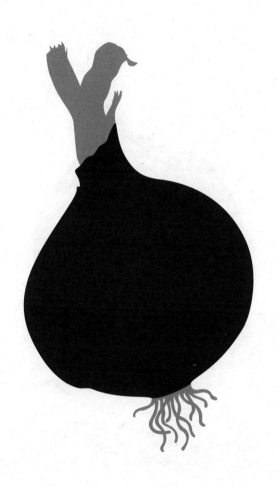

NOTES

Music encroached on this book. Phrases from Joni Mitchell's "Big Yellow Taxi," Icona Pop's "I Love It," The Bangles' "Walk Like an Egyptian" (I do not condone the weird race politics of this song) and "(Get Your Kicks On) Route 66" (a standard of rhythm and blues composed by Bobby Troup) all found a place. "I Want a Prime Minister Who Cries" is wall-to-wall nineties musical references and why should I ruin it by listing them?

The streets and establishments referred to throughout (Robson, Park Lane, Liverpool, York, etc.) can be found in Halifax, Vancouver, Montreal, Edmonton or Fredericton. Their locations are usually clarified by other contextual details of each poem.

My friend Coral Short is the (brilliant) performance artist mentioned in the second portion of the book's first poem.

In "Psych Ward Grub," "Sandra Lee" refers to Sandra Lee of the television program *Semi-Homemade with Sandra Lee* in which the host, Sandra Lee, uses a seventy/thirty ratio of prepackaged to fresh foods in order to prepare meals. In the same poem, "Rene Redzepi" refers to Rene Redzepi, head chef of Copenhagen restaurant Noma, known for hyper-local Nordic cuisine.

You probably already know that the title of "It's Like We Have ESPN or Something" is adapted from the screenplay of a special teen film known as *Mean Girls*.

The chef referred to in "Theses on the Hydrology of Sweet Tea" is Heston Blumenthal.

"Essential Oils and Precious Metals" includes quotations from Sylvia Plath's "Daddy" and Gertrude Stein's "Susie Asado."

Otherwise, I will refrain from explaining every allusion or obscurity to better preserve your reading pleasure.

ACKNOWLEDGEMENTS

Thank you to Amber McMillan and Silas White of Nightwood Editions for your support. Thank you to Carleton Wilson for the gorgeous cover design.

Some poems in this collection were previously published in *The Walrus, Chelsea Station, Room, Prairie Fire, PRISM International, Dreamland, The New Quarterly, Atlantis* and *Rampike*. Thank you to the editors and readers of these publications.

I thank certain of my friends—Derek Warwick, Marco Katz Montiel, Nathan Strayed and Jane Komori—who each workshopped a poem or two with me. You are all talented writers in your own right, but more importantly, you are wonderful people.

I survived some of my more harrowing times (from which some of these poems take their cue) due to the support of Carmen Ellison.

Thank you to Jennifer Crawford, Joan Crawford, Sebastian Kennickell and Triny Finlay. I love you all.

ABOUT THE AUTHOR

Lucas Crawford was born in Halifax, raised in rural Nova Scotia, currently lives in Fredericton and is associate professor of English at the University of New Brunswick. Crawford is the author of two previous poetry books: *Sideshow Concessions* (Invisible Publishing, 2015), winner of the 2015 Robert Kroetsch Award for Innovative Poetry, and *The High Line Scavenger Hunt* (University of Calgary Press, 2018). In August 2019, Manhattan's High Line park launched a poetry-based audio guide for its visitors based on Crawford's second poetry book and the work of two other artists.